The Stor
Birling Gap

Birling Gap is an idyllic coastal hamlet nestled between the Seven Sisters and Beachy Head.

With a National Trust café, shop, visitor centre and steps down to the sea, it is popular all year round whatever the weather.

It has witnessed invasion, smugglers, ship-wrecks, coastal erosion and a great many tourists flock to its beach.

This is the story of Birling Gap.

by Rob Wassell

RAW
Publications

The Story of
Birling Gap

Published by RAW Publications
www.rawpublications.co.uk

First printed November 2017

International Standard Book Number
ISBN 978-0-9569912-4-9

RAW
Publications
www.rawpublications.co.uk

NN405 'Sharlisa'
Now relocated due to ongoing coastal erosion

Coastguard Cottages, Rocket House, Lookout and Perimeter Wall in 1911

Birling Gap with wooden steps to the beach, circa 1960

Birling Gap

The gap between the towering chalk cliffs at Birling was an obvious place for invaders to land.

In 43AD the Romans invaded and settled. It wasn't until later that the 'Beorls' were to give Birling Gap its name. A war-like tribe of Saxon sea rovers, they harassed the coast of Sussex before settling outside of what is modern Eastbourne in 489AD.

William the Conqueror travelled through this way and it was his half-brother Robert, Earl of Mortain, who eventually came into possession of Birling.

It passed into the hands of the Bardolph family who stayed for two hundred years until they lost Birling after the Wars of the Roses.

From 1565, Birling was held by the Carew family for over 100 years. It then passed through various owners until 1807 when it was acquired by Charles Gilbert.

By 1817, it had been handed down to his niece, Mary Anne Gilbert who went on to marry Davies Giddy, then president of the Royal Society.

The manor of Birling has remained part of the Davies-Gilbert estate ever since.

Birling Gap, November 2007

Cliff fall at the Seven Sisters, May 2016

The Chalk Cliffs

The white chalk cliffs at Birling Gap were formed between 65 and 100 million years ago when the land was completely covered by a warm sea.

The cliffs are the remains of coccoliths: plankton, that died and sank to the bottom. Compressed over time, they now form the dense, yet porous, rock that covers much of the South East.

The land between England and France was once a fertile low-lying tundra. At the end of the last Ice Age, approximately 10,000 years ago, the area flooded with meltwater from the North Sea, thus creating the English Channel.

The pounding waves, wind, rain and icy winters take their toll on the fragile cliffs. Cracks become cavities, which in turn become fissures, which in-evitably lead to a fall.

In May 2016, the largest fall for over ten years occurred when part of the Seven Sisters was lost to the sea. The resulting boulders form tempo-rary barriers which help protect the cliff from the waves, until they wash away and the cycle begins again. This rate of erosion continues at an aver-age of 60 centimetres per year.

Nympha Americana, 1747

Coonatto, 1876

SS Eastfield, 1909 (and below)

Shipwrecks

The coastline off Birling Gap is notorious for its unpredictable currents and dangerous rocky shoreline. Outcrops of flint-encrusted chalk have caused hundreds of shipwrecks over centuries.

Nympha Americana, 1747

Britain was at war with Spain and the ship was captured as a prize by Commander George Walker. It was laden with gold, silver, lace, velvets, silks, coins and mercury. It was caught in a storm and ran aground near the Seven Sisters. Despite much of the cargo being looted, Thomas Fletcher, the local excise officer, managed to protect some of the goods and return them to their owners.

The Coonatto, 1876

A 633 ton fast clipper, built specifically for the Australian wool and tea trade, it ran aground on the 21st February, returning from Adelaide laden with copper ingots and wool.

The Eastfield, 1909

A 2,300 ton steamer, it ran aground during a storm on its return trip from Borneo. It was successfully refloated three weeks later during a high tide.

The UB-121 beside the Oushla in 1920

The Oushla and UB-121

German Submarine UB-121

The Comptesse De Flandre in 1925

Oushla, 1916

The Oushla was a steam driven ship, constructed in Sunderland in 1891. She was en route to Liverpool from London and was unladen. A strong south-westerly gale and her light weight brought her ashore right up against the chalk cliffs near Crowlink. The crew were able to walk off and were given shelter at the Birling Gap Hotel.

UB-121, 1920

The UB-121 was a German type III submarine that was built in 1918. It was surrendered at the end of the First World War. While under tow with two other U-Boats, they broke their moorings. One sank near Beachy Head, another washed up in Hastings and the UB-121 came to rest at Birling Gap alongside the Oushla.

Comptesse de Flandre, 1925

The Comptesse de Flandre was hit by a fierce storm whilst carrying a large cargo of goods between Naples, Italy and London. A lifeboat and tug boat attended with all 27 members of the crew rescued by rope and line from boat to cliff-top.

These wrecks became a popular tourist attraction, encouraging many visitors to Birling Gap.

East Dean by William Lambert, circa 1780

Illustration of the cave from 1926

Two boys beneath Parson Darby's hole in 1899   Remains of the cave in 1938

Reverend Jonathan Darby

In 1706, Jonathan Darby took up his role as Parson of the Parish of East Dean. He was deeply concerned at having to bury sailors' bodies washed ashore and especially so when an 800-ton schooner ran aground with the loss of all of her crew.

A petition for a lighthouse had been agreed but nothing had yet been done about its construction.

Parson Darby decided to take matters into his own hands by hollowing out an old smugglers' cave situated 20 feet above the high water mark. Originally used as a store for contraband, it is from here that Parson Darby shone a light on stormy nights and helped to save countless sailors' lives.

Parson Darby died on the 26th October 1726 and his grave in East Dean churchyard reads: 'Here lies the body of Parson Darby. He was the sailors' friend.'

Even after Parson Darby's passing, the cave continued to save lives with a report from 1870 when the cave afforded refuge to a crew of 12.

In Victorian times the cave attracted many tourists. It was sketched and painted and its features were still partly visible up to the 1970s.

Belle Tout operational, pre 1900

Belle Tout with lens curtain, circa 1900

Belle Tout, decommissioned 1909

Belle Tout part-destroyed, 1940s

Moving Belle Tout in 1999

The Belle Tout Lighthouse, now a unique bed and breakfast

The Belle Tout Lighthouse

In 1832, work started on a permanent lighthouse.

On the 11th October 1834 the light first shone, although its cliff-top location meant it was often obscured by mist and erosion threatened its future.

By the late 1800s the decision had been made to abandon Belle Tout and build a new lighthouse.

In 1902 Belle Tout was decomissioned and sold to Mr. Davies-Gilbert who ran it as a tea house.

In 1923 it was purchased by Sir James Purves-Stewart who remodelled it as a stately home.

Evacuated during the war, the lighthouse was used for gunnery practice by Canadian troops who left it in ruins. Sir James was horrified and gifted the remains to Eastbourne Corporation.

Belle Tout was lovingly restored by the Cullinan family, used by the BBC to film 'The Life and Loves of a She-Devil' and moved 15 metres from the crumbling cliff edge by Ihe Roberts family in 1999.

Rob Wassell's Trust tried to buy Belle Tout in 2007.

David and Barbara Shaw bought the building in 2008 and have turned it into a unique B&B.

Lighthouse foundations and platform, 1901

The journey to work, 1901

Lighthouse part constructed, 1901

Postcard dated 1927

Cleaning the lens

Lighting the lamp, 1972

New stripes, 2013

The Beachy Head Lighthouse

In 1900, Trinity House embarked on an ambitious task - to build a new lighthouse at the base of the cliffs. Its inaccessibility inspired a genius idea - to build a ropeway to ferry masonry and men direct from the cliff-top to the platform 550ft below.

Built using Cornish granite, the tower is 141ft (43m) high, with eight separate levels, including entrance, oil tanks, crane room, storage area, living quarters, bedrooms, watch room and lantern room. The light had a range of 16 miles and came into operation on the 2nd October 1902.

The original lighthouse had a black stripe painted on grey granite and it wasn't until 1951 that the black stripe was painted red to help it stand out.

There were three keepers 'on station' who worked in shifts to ensure that the light didn't go out.

In 1975 the lighthouse was switched over to electricity. In 1980 the lighthouse was painted red and white. In 1983 the lighthouse was automated.

In 2011 the Save the Stripes campaign successfully raised money to re-paint the lighthouse which was completed on the 10th October 2013.

An eight-oared rowing galley running contraband ashore

A Revenue cutter chasing a smuggling vessel

Smuggling

Smuggling in Britain was at its height in the 1700s and 1800s. Smugglers illegally brought goods such as tea, tobacco and gin into Britain to avoid paying tax of up to 30% which helped pay for costly wars such as the Napoleonic War (1799-1815).

A night's work from smuggling was often worth more than a month's wage for a farm labourer. As many workers struggled to earn enough to feed themselves and their families, smuggling provided an alternative, yet dangerous, means of income. If caught, a smuggler could be imprisoned, con-scripted into the navy or even executed.

Smugglers relied on a network of support from local communities. Some local houses such as Crowlink House, and churches, including Jeving-ton, were reputedly used to hide smuggled goods on their route from the coast to inland towns.

The coastguard station at Birling Gap was first built in 1817 to help support the coastguards stationed at Eastbourne, Crowlink and Cuckmere Haven.

By the 1840s smuggling had declined after an increase in coastguard responsibility and also sig-nificantly reduced tax on imported goods.

V1 Flying Bomb or 'Doodle Bug' over Cuckmere Haven, 1944

"I well remember the night we first saw the doo-dle-bugs. We spotted these lights in the sky and had no idea what they might be."

Two sentries, armed with rifles and a Bren gun at Birling Gap, 28th October 1940

The Second World War

Birling Gap was like 'Clapham Junction of the Air'.

The first bombs fell on 7th July 1940 and a U-Boat shelled Cuckmere Haven on the 31st August.

Most inhabitants were evacuated and civilian access to the area was restricted. Canadian troops were stationed at Birling Gap and the gunnery ranges near Belle Tout where they infamously tested their ammunition on the walls of the lighthouse.

The beach had obstructions to prevent landings. Concrete blocks called 'Dragon's Teeth' were used as anti-tank defences and some of these can still be seen in East Dean and Cuckmere Haven.

Emergency airfields were constructed along the coast, including one at Friston, together with radar, artillery positions and monitoring stations.

Birling Gap saw a lot of action. The Battle of Britain was fought directly overhead. There were day and night 'hit and run' raids which continued up to 1942. Night bombings took place between 1943 and 1944. From June to August 1944 the V1 flying bombs flew overhead, hit the cliff or were deflected from their London targets by fighter planes.

Birling Gap Coastguard Station, Eastbourne Chronicle, 8th June 1951

Cottage demolition, Eastbourne Gazette, 28th December 1994

The remaining four Coastguard Cottages, 10th April 2014

The Coastguard Cottages

In 1878 the Admiralty built eight cottages at Birling Gap for the Coastguard.

In 1951 the cottages passed into private ownership but the coastguard continued to man a station on the top of the cliff to aid sea and cliff-top rescues.

In 1973 the first cottage was demolished by the council due to its closeness to the cliff edge.

In 1994 the second cottage was taken down with calls from residents for cliff protection ignored.

The Birling Gap Cliff Protection Association formed in 1996 to try to save the remaining cottages - a proposal which was rejected.

In March 2002 another cottage was demolished when the distance from the cliff was reduced to 10ft.

A further cottage was demolished in March 2014 leaving just four of the original cottages remaining.

"We believe sea defences are not a sustainable solution. Our policy is always to go with natural processes and allow them to take their course. At Birling Gap, we will continue to manage the site within those natural processes," said Jonathan Light of the National Trust.

The Birling Gap Hotel in 1981

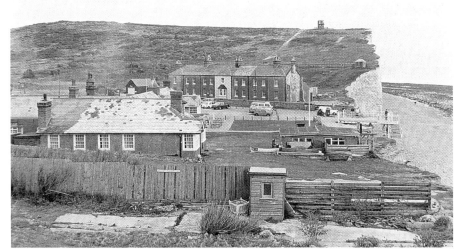

The Birling Gap Hotel in 1986 and below in 1994

The Birling Gap Hotel

The hotel was built in the 1880s and was a Victorian colonial style villa, later with a 1930's interior.

During the war, the hotel was taken over by the Canadians and the kitchens used to prepare meals.

Some of the houses were commandeered for NCOs and local troops, while the artillery units, who practised on the firing ranges near Belle Tout, ate in specially constructed huts on the site.

The Collins family ran the Hotel from 1958 and carried out extensive renovations. Known for serving locally caught fresh fish every day, the hotel was often fully booked for food and lodging.

The Birling Gap Hotel, Eastbourne Gazette, 20th January, 1993

The National Trust took over the management of the Birling Gap Hotel on 20th April 2010.

The safety boat being launched by winch from the cliff top, circa 1985

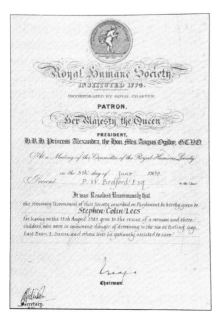

The Humane Society Testimonial

The safety boat being launched

The Birling Gap Safety Boat

On the 19th September 1983, Graham Collins of the Birling Gap Hotel was alerted when a man got into difficulties in the sea. Graham fought his way through the worsening conditions and rescued him. For this act of bravery he received the Royal Humane Society's Testimonial printed on vellum.

It was this event that inspired the idea for a safety boat to be located at Birling Gap and a charity was officially registered on 14th September 1984.

The safety boat carried out many rescues, including assisting the Coastguard and the Lifeboat. The organisation also searched for missing persons and gave safety talks and demonstrations.

The safety boat assisted in other operations and the filming of TV adverts and films, including Robin Hood Prince of Thieves at Cuckmere.

The boathouse was demolished in 2014, as erosion threatened its cliff-top location and to prevent parts of the building falling on people below.

The charity no longer had a location from which to launch the safety boat so it was officially wound up on the 9th June 2016.

Steps cut out from the chalk cliff, 1934

Removing the steps prior to cottage demolition, Eastbourne Herald, January 1994

Eastbourne Herald, January 1994

Gazette, 20th July 1994

The Steps to the Beach

At its lowest point, the cliff at Birling Gap is only around 30 feet high and steps were originally carved out of the chalk to access the beach.

The National Trust have designed the current steps so they can be moved easily to keep pace with the constant process of coastal erosion.

The steps were repositioned in 1994, with access being closed between January and July until the new steps were installed in place and re-opened.

The steps have had to be moved again since, with the most recent relocation in October 2017.

The steps at Birling Gap, 25th March 2016

July 2007

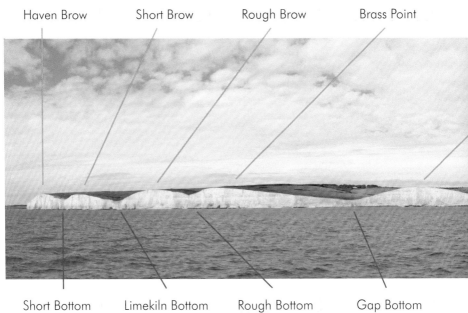

Haven Brow   Short Brow   Rough Brow   Brass Point

Short Bottom   Limekiln Bottom   Rough Bottom   Gap Bottom

The Seven Sisters

The prominent hills and dips of the chalk cliffs between Cuckmere Haven and Birling Gap all have names. The original Seven Sisters now count as eight due to erosion dividing two of the hills.

Flagstaff Brow   Flat Brow   Baily's Hill   Went Hill

Flagstaff Bottom   Flat Hill Bottom   Michel Dean   Birling Gap

Birling Gap and the Seven Sisters, postcard dated 1935

Birling Gap and the Seven Sisters, postcard dated 1953

Birling Gap and the Seven Sisters, postcard circa 1960

Birling Gap and the Seven Sisters, postcard dated 1968

January 2016

Pencil drawing by John Graham of Birling Gap in September 1832

Territorial units, Scouts and clubs held annual camps at Birling Gap, 1930s

The beach with steps cut into the chalk. Each year they would be refashioned by the Gilbert Estate, 1930s

The Chief Coast-guard's house in 1973

Birling Gap with the Old Golf Clubhouse on the left, circa 1976

The Coastguard Cottages, later named Crangon Cottages, with Rocket House
in foreground and Lookout Office near the cliff edge, 1920s

Wooden removable steps were used to replace the previous steps which collapsed.
Ramp used to launch a fishing boat from the cliff, The Argus, 12th February 1970

Hotel on the left in 1986 with Coastguard Tower on the hill, demolished in 1991

June 2016

Looking Eastwards, a photograph by Louis Levy circa 1906

Looking Westwards, a postcard from the 1930s

Looking Eastwards, June 2016

Looking Westwards, September 2016

National Trust café, shop and visitor centre, 25th March 2016

Birling Gap, a very popular tourist destination, 25th March 2016

The National Trust

The charity was founded in 1895 and works to preserve and protect the nation's heritage and open spaces, including forests, archaelogical remains, historic houses, gardens, mills and coastline.

In 1982 the National Trust purchased Birling Gap, including the hotel, the car park and some downland - six acres in total which brought the Trust's holding in the area to 638 acres.

The original hotel building has been remodelled to include a café, shop and an informative visitor centre. The car parks have been improved with plenty of space for the hundreds of thousands of visitors that are drawn to Birling Gap each year.

The National Trust have carried out archaeological surveys, run special events and continue to inform visitors about the area's fascinating history.

The National Trust works with the natural processes that constantly change the coastline to provide continued enjoyment to Birling Gap's many admirers.

www.nationaltrust.org.uk

Birling Gap with the Belle Tout Lighthouse in the distance, 5th June 2016

There is something very special about Birling Gap. Nestled between the Seven Sisters and Beachy Head, it is a timeless and magical place.

In 2007 I tried to buy the Belle Tout Lighthouse by public subscription and you can find out more about the history of this fascinating building in my book, 'The Story of the Belle Tout Lighthouse' ISBN 978-0-9569912-0-1. I am delighted to still be involved with Belle Tout to this day.

I also did my bit to help Save the Stripes of the iconic red and white lighthouse at the base of the cliffs in 'The Story of the Beachy Head Lighthouse' ISBN 978-0-9569912-1-8.

Thank you to Heather for her love and unending support and my friend Tina for her input and proof-reading.

Rob Wassell

Visit www.birlinggapsussex.co.uk for more information.

All photography, writing and content by Rob Wassell unless otherwise credited.

Many of the old photographs and postcards I have acquired over the years and some of their origins are unknown. My apologies If I have failed to give credit, I have not done so on purpose and will gladly correct this in future if brought to my attention.

With special thanks to the National Trust at Birling Gap for their help and support with some of the material included within this book.

https://www.nationaltrust.org.uk/birling-gap-and-the-seven-sisters

Credits:

Page 4 - Wooden Steps to the Beach, The Francis Frith Collection

Page 8 - Nympha Americana Copyright Royal Museum Greenwich

Page 12 - Cave Illustration from History with a Sketch Book by Donald Maxwell, 1926

Page 14 - Moving of the Belle Tout Lighthouse, courtesy of The Argus

Page 16 - Photographs of the lighthouse keepers, courtesy of the ALK and Kath Clarke's Grandfather, Alfred George May's photo of the construction of the Beachy Head Lighthouse.

Page 20 - Two Sentries Licensed for print by the Imperial War Museum picture library.

Page 24 - Aerial photo by Terry Connolly, Eastbourne Gazette, 2nd February 1994

Page 26 - Material from the original BGSBA website and other sources.

Page 28 - Carved chalk steps © Historic England. Licensor canmore.org.uk

Additional credits to: Eastbourne Library, Seaford Library, University of Sussex, Eastbourne Herald & Gazette, Beachy Head and East Dean and Friston by John Surtees and other sources.